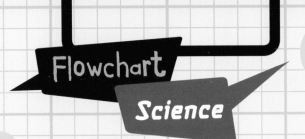

Flowchart
Science

The DIGESTIVE SYSTEM

Richard and Louise Spilsbury

raintree
a Capstone company — publishers for children

Raintree is an imprint of Capstone Global Library Limited, a company incorporated in England and Wales having its registered office at 264 Banbury Road, Oxford, OX2 7DY – Registered company number: 6695582

www.raintree.co.uk
myorders@raintree.co.uk

Produced for Raintree by Calcium
Editors: Sarah Eason and Harriet McGregor
Designers: Paul Myerscough and Simon Borrough
Picture researcher: Rachel Bloun
Originated by Capstone Global Library Limited © 2018

ISBN 978 1 4747 6581 7 (hardback)
22 21 20 19 18
10 9 8 7 6 5 4 3 2 1

ISBN 978 1 4747 6596 1 (paperback)
23 22 21 20 19
10 9 8 7 6 5 4 3 2 1

British Library Cataloguing in Publication Data
A full catalogue record for this book is available from the British Library.

Acknowledgements
Cover art: Shutterstock: Denk Creative; Simon Borrough.
Picture credits: Shutterstock: 3445128471 35, Alila Medical Media 31, Ashusha 23, Joe Belanger 21, Samuel Borges Photography 38–39, Chombosan 20, Cliparea/Custom Media 26, Devenorr 33, Dimarion 27, Extender_01 29, La Gorda 5, Gosphotodesign 4, Ramona Kaulitzki 37, Sebastian Kaulitzki 32, Kazoka 45, Kateryna Kon 19t, 41, Maya Kruchankova 1, 10, Leolintang 12, Madlen 44–45, Maradon 333 6–7, Mmutlu 18–19, Monkey Business Images 11, 24–25, Negovura 14, Nerthuz 12–13, Tyler Olson 30, Power best 6, Ra3rn 16, RedlineVector 43, Elena Schweitzer 38, Tefi 34, Tomacco 9, Bo Valentino 40, Luna Vandoorne 17.

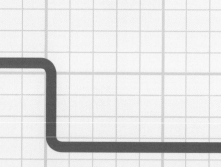

Printed and bound in China.

Contents

Chapter 1   Breaking it down! 4

Chapter 2   The digestive system 10

Chapter 3   Digestion at work 16

Chapter 4   How the body uses food 24

Chapter 5   Waste 30

Chapter 6   Improving digestion 38

Glossary 46

Find out more 47

Index 48

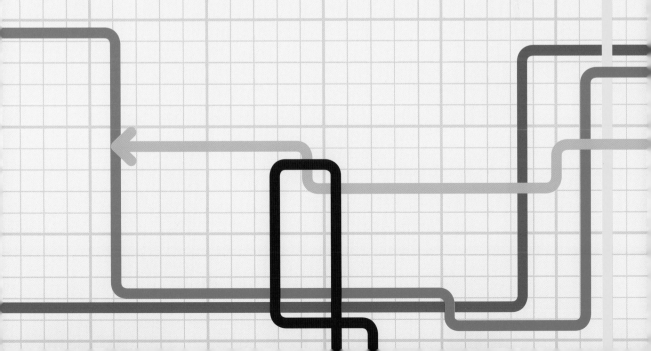

Chapter 1
Breaking it down!

Each year, your body processes hundreds of kilograms of food. First you chew your food, then it passes through the digestive system. The digestive system is a series of pipes, tubes and organs. This complex system breaks down the food into fuel and materials that your body uses to live, work and grow.

Your digestive system is about 9 metres (30 feet) long from end to end, which is almost as long as a bus!

Food provides the nutrients needed to build and fuel the body. To use the nutrients, the body must first break them down into very tiny pieces that can dissolve in liquid. Then the blood can transport the pieces around the body, delivering the different substances.

When the body digests food it takes the parts that are useful and it separates these out from parts that it does not need or that could be damaging. This is waste. The excretory system is part of the digestive system. It keeps us healthy by removing these waste materials. Waste passes from the digestive to the excretory system and out of the body.

The organs of the digestive system are shown here. The system begins with the mouth.

Get smart!

The time it takes for the body to digest a meal varies. It can depend on what has been eaten. Some food is digested within a few hours. Other foods take days to be fully broken down, sorted and passed through the pipework of the digestive system.

Food is fuel

The digestive system changes food into a mushy liquid. It breaks down food and drink into smaller pieces of carbohydrates, proteins, fats and vitamins. These are the substances that the body needs to survive and to stay healthy.

Carbohydrates are broken down by the process of digestion into sugars. People need sugars for **energy**. Carbohydrates are found in a lot of foods such as wholegrain breads and cereals, and fruit and vegetables. Foods such as meat, eggs and beans contain molecules of protein that the body breaks down into even smaller molecules. These can be used for building and repairing body parts.

Cars usually run on petrol or diesel fuel. Food is the fuel that humans need.

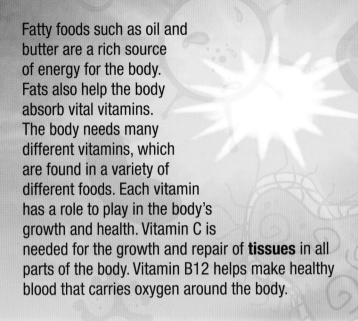

Fatty foods such as oil and butter are a rich source of energy for the body. Fats also help the body absorb vital vitamins. The body needs many different vitamins, which are found in a variety of different foods. Each vitamin has a role to play in the body's growth and health. Vitamin C is needed for the growth and repair of **tissues** in all parts of the body. Vitamin B12 helps make healthy blood that carries oxygen around the body.

Plants need sunlight to make food. When people eat plants, their bodies convert that food into fuel and energy.

Get smart!

On Earth, we get energy from sunlight. Plants make their own food in a process called photosynthesis. The plants' green parts capture energy in sunlight. They use this energy to combine water and carbon dioxide, a gas in the air, to make a sugar called glucose. Plants use some of the glucose to live and grow. They store the rest as **starch** in their roots and other parts for future use. People eat plants and plant-eating animals to get energy themselves.

Get flow chart smart!

Digesting food

This flow chart shows what happens in the digestive system.

The food we eat passes through the digestive system, which is about 9 metres (30 feet) long.

The digestive system breaks food down into very tiny pieces the body can use.

Undigested food and waste passes from the digestive to the excretory system and out of the body.

Blood transports nutrients around the body.

Carbohydrates are broken down into sugars needed for energy.

→

Protein is digested into smaller molecules used for building and repairing body parts.

↓

Vitamins help the body to grow and stay healthy.

←

Fats supply energy and help the body absorb vitamins.

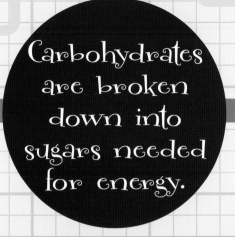

Flowchart Smart

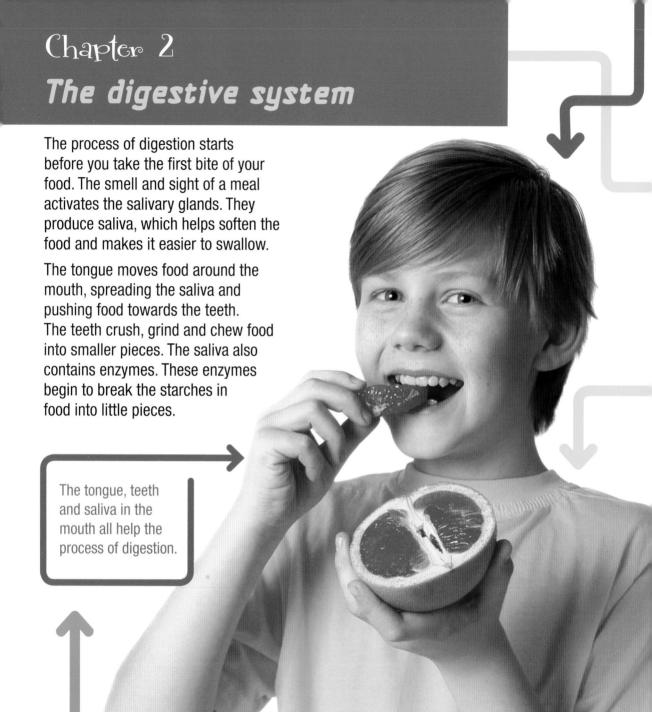

Chapter 2
The digestive system

The process of digestion starts before you take the first bite of your food. The smell and sight of a meal activates the salivary glands. They produce saliva, which helps soften the food and makes it easier to swallow.

The tongue moves food around the mouth, spreading the saliva and pushing food towards the teeth. The teeth crush, grind and chew food into smaller pieces. The saliva also contains enzymes. These enzymes begin to break the starches in food into little pieces.

The tongue, teeth and saliva in the mouth all help the process of digestion.

If we see and smell something tasty, our senses tell the body to get ready to digest some food.

Have you ever gulped food quickly and felt it go down the wrong way? At the back of your throat there is a windpipe, which lets air in and out when you breathe. When you swallow, a flap called the epiglottis covers the opening of the windpipe. This keeps food from entering the windpipe. If the epiglottis does not have time to close, some food or drink can go down the windpipe instead. You cough when this happens as your body tries to clear the windpipe.

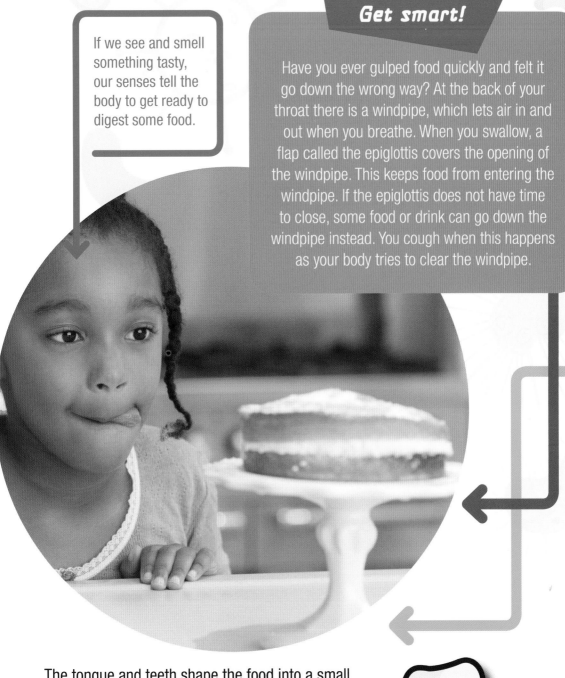

The tongue and teeth shape the food into a small ball shape called a bolus. Then the tongue moves the bolus to the back of the throat and into the opening of the oesophagus. The oesophagus is a tube about 25 centimetres (10 inches) long. The oesophagus moves food from the back of the throat to the stomach in a couple of seconds.

11

Stomach and intestines

Although digesting and swallowing food is quite a quick job, food takes longer to pass through the stomach. It typically stays in the stomach for up to 6 hours before it moves into the intestines.

When food enters the stomach, a ring of muscle at the bottom of the oesophagus squeezes tight to stop the food getting out again. The stomach stores the food, breaks it down and then slowly empties it into the **small intestine**. The small intestine absorbs about 90 per cent of the nutrients and water from the food as it passes through. Then the **large intestine** absorbs any remaining useful parts before finally removing the waste.

The different pipes through which food passes on its long journey in the digestive system are collectively known as the **alimentary canal**. The walls of the alimentary canal contain muscles. These muscles squeeze behind the food to force it forwards, and then relax. This muscle action is how the alimentary canal moves food along, and it is called **peristalsis**. The alimentary canal begins at the mouth, where food enters the body, and ends with the anus, where solid wastes are expelled.

If you eat too much too quickly, your stomach can feel uncomfortable as it struggles to contain and digest the food.

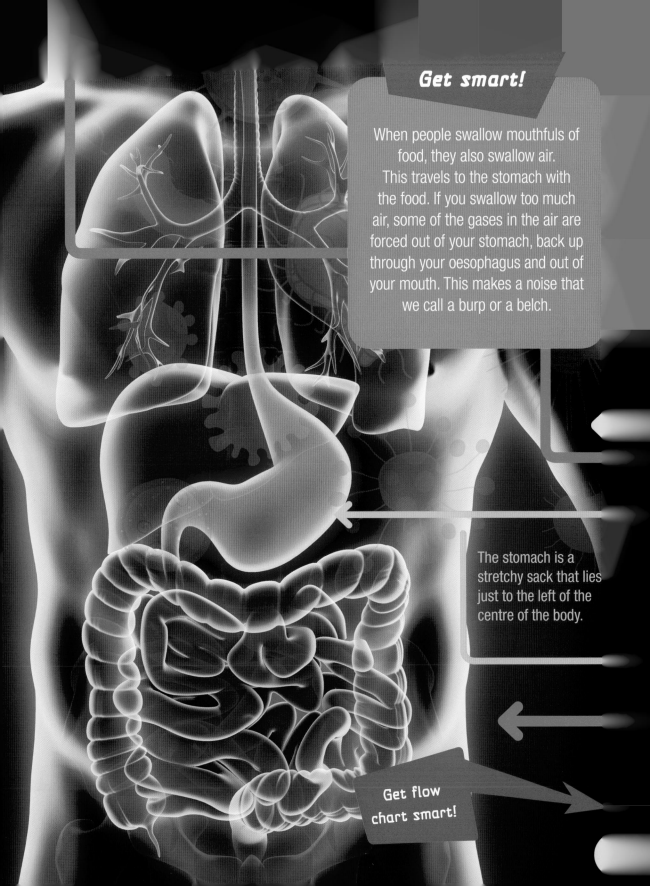

Get smart!

When people swallow mouthfuls of food, they also swallow air. This travels to the stomach with the food. If you swallow too much air, some of the gases in the air are forced out of your stomach, back up through your oesophagus and out of your mouth. This makes a noise that we call a burp or a belch.

The stomach is a stretchy sack that lies just to the left of the centre of the body.

Get flow chart smart!

Food's journey

Follow the steps in this flow chart to learn about the route food takes through the digestive system.

When people see and smell food, the salivary glands produce saliva in the mouth.

Saliva softens the food and begins to break down any starches.

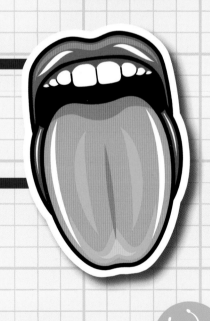

The large intestine absorbs any remaining useful parts before removing the waste.

The tongue moves food to the teeth, which crush, grind and chew it up into small pieces.

The tongue and the teeth shape the food into a bolus, which the tongue moves into the oesophagus.

The stomach stores food, breaks it down, and empties it into the small intestine.

The oesophagus moves food from the back of the throat to the stomach.

The small intestine absorbs about 90 per cent of nutrients and water from the food.

Flowchart

Smart

15

Chapter 3

Digestion at work

The stomach mixes and blends food to break it down. It also produces liquids to help dissolve food. There are liquids called acids in the stomach that are strong enough to dissolve metal.

Strong muscles in the walls of the stomach squeeze the stomach to make it mix the food that comes from the oesophagus. This is called churning. The inner layer of the stomach is covered with wrinkles called gastric folds. These help grip and move food during digestion and they also allow the stomach to stretch and make space for a large meal. Gradually, the stomach churning breaks the balls of food into smaller and smaller pieces until they form a mushy mixture called chyme.

Muscles squeeze to move food through the alimentary canal just as we squeeze toothpaste to move it through the tube.

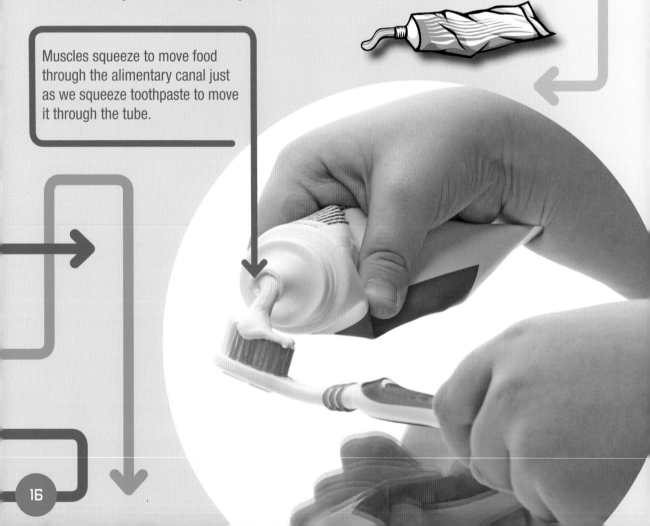

The stomach works a little like a food blender. It breaks down food into mushy lumps.

Get smart!

Have you ever wondered why your stomach sometimes makes rumbles and growls? These noises happen as food, fluid and gases move and churn through the stomach and intestines. When the stomach and intestines are nearly empty the noises sound louder because there is nothing inside the organs to muffle the sound.

Gastric juices help the stomach break down food. These juices are released by special glands in the lining of the stomach. They contain enzymes that help break down the protein in foods such as meat. Glands also produce acids, which help kill bacteria that may be in the food. Bacteria are tiny living things and some can cause disease. The glands release about 0.5 litres (1 pint) of gastric juice after a big meal to aid digestion. In 24 hours your stomach produces about 2–3 litres (3.5–4 pints) of gastric juices!

Into the small intestine

The mix of partially digested food and digestive juices called chyme leaves the stomach and enters the small intestine. On average, the small intestine is about 6 metres (20 feet) long and about 2.5 centimetres (1 inch) wide.

Food stays in the small intestine for about 4 hours. More enzymes and acids are added to the chyme and the process of chemical digestion continues, breaking down molecules of food into smaller ones. For example, some food particles are broken down into glucose, the sugar the body uses for energy, in the small intestine. When the food particles are small enough, they are absorbed by the thousands of tiny villi that line the wall of the small intestine. Villi are tiny folds that stick out from the intestinal wall like lots of little fingers, pointing towards the centre.

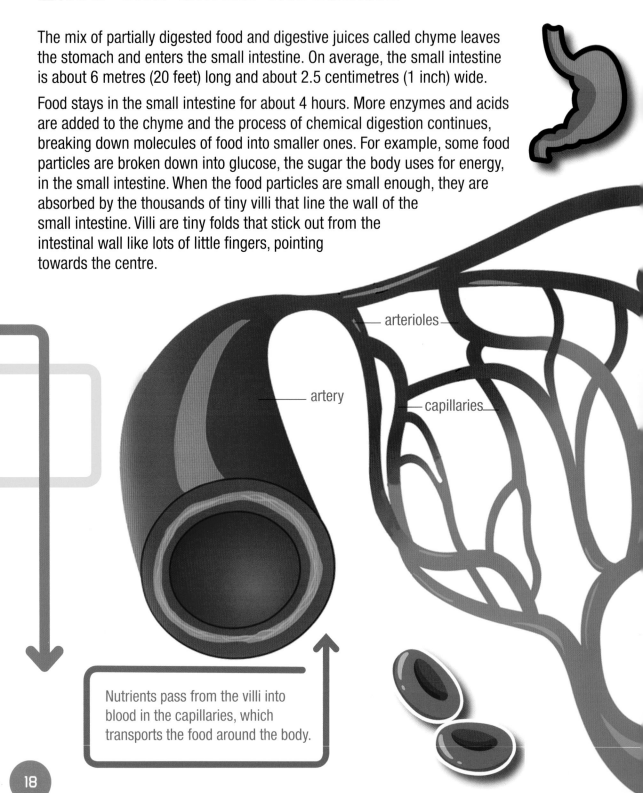

arterioles

artery

capillaries

Nutrients pass from the villi into blood in the capillaries, which transports the food around the body.

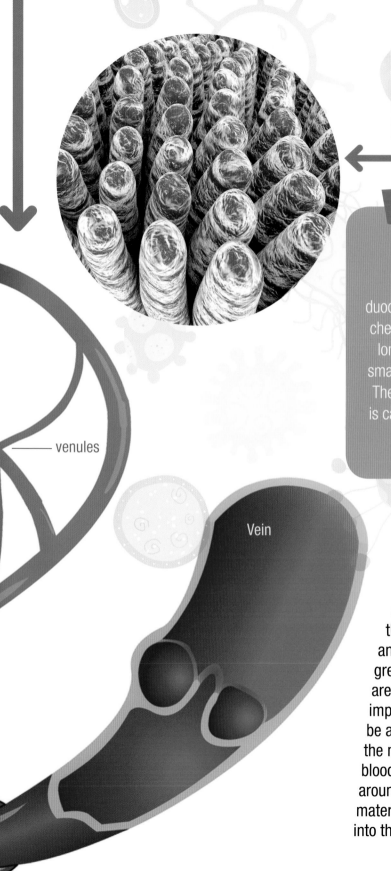

Villi are so small they can only be seen through a microscope.

Get smart!

The first part of the small intestine is called the duodenum. This is where most of the chemical digestion takes place. The long, coiled middle section of the small intestine is called the jejunum. The final part of the small intestine is called the ileum and this is where any remaining nutrients are absorbed.

venules

Vein

Inside the villi there are capillaries, which are very tiny blood vessels. Vitamins and nutrients pass through the very thin walls of the villi and into the capillaries. The villi greatly increase the total surface area of the intestine walls. This improves how quickly nutrients can be absorbed. Once in the capillaries, the nutrients move along in the bloodstream and are transported around the body. Any remaining food material in the small intestine passes into the large intestine.

Helping digestion

The small intestine does not work alone. It is helped by the liver, gall bladder and pancreas. Food does not pass through all of these organs during digestion, but they all provide the small intestine with chemicals it needs to carry out digestion.

The liver is the largest internal organ. In an adult, it is about the size of a football. It is located mainly in the upper right part of the abdomen above the stomach and below the diaphragm. The liver produces bile. Bile is a brown-green digestive juice that helps break up fatty foods. The liver stores bile in the gall bladder, a pear-shaped organ located just below the liver. When the body needs more bile to help digest food, the gall bladder releases it into the intestine.

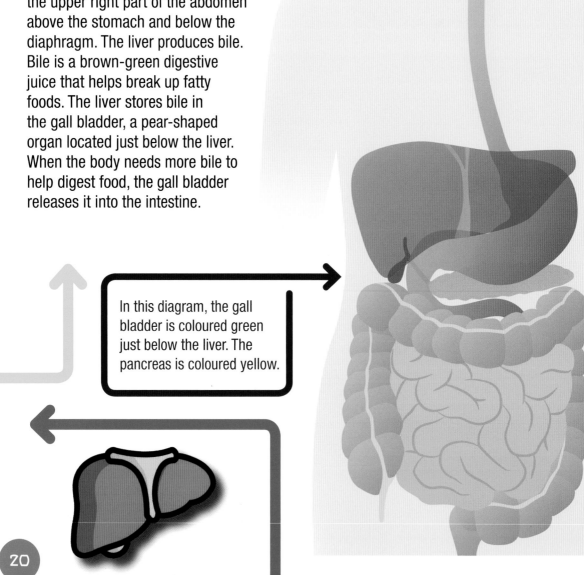

In this diagram, the gall bladder is coloured green just below the liver. The pancreas is coloured yellow.

The first of the three sections of the small intestine, the duodenum, produces large quantities of mucus. This slimy substance coats the walls of the small intestine to help food move along smoothly and easily. It also helps protect the intestinal lining from acid in the chyme.

The pancreas is about 18 centimetres (7 inches) long and is located just behind the stomach. The pancreas produces pancreatic juice. When we eat, the pancreas releases this enzyme-rich juice into the duodenum. The enzymes help break down fats, proteins and carbohydrates. The juice also helps neutralize the acidic gastric juices, which would otherwise damage the lining of the intestine.

Bile breaks down fats in the food we eat a little like washing-up liquid breaking up oil and fat on dirty plates.

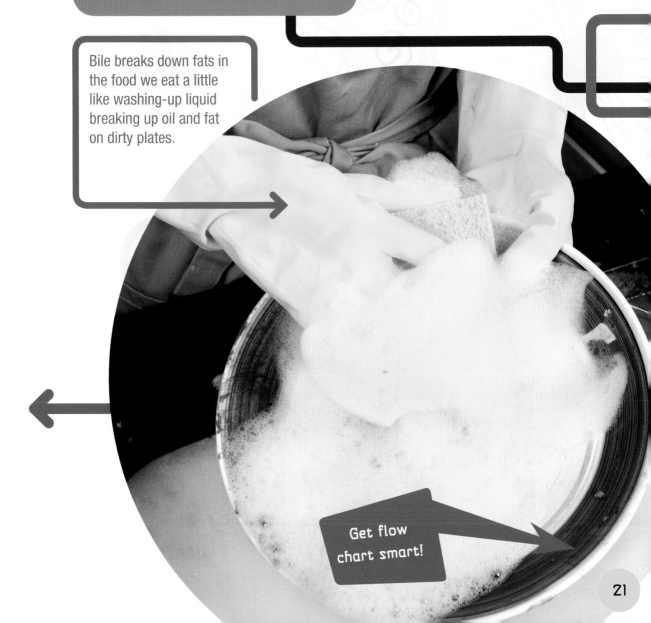

Get flow chart smart!

The stomach and intestines

The steps in this flow chart explain how the stomach and intestines digest food.

Muscles in the stomach walls stretch to fit in all the food eaten in a meal.

The muscles squeeze to churn and break up the food in the stomach. Enzymes help the stomach break down food.

Nutrients pass through the very thin villi walls into the capillaries. They are transported around the body in the bloodstream.

When food particles are small enough, they are absorbed into villi that line the small intestine walls.

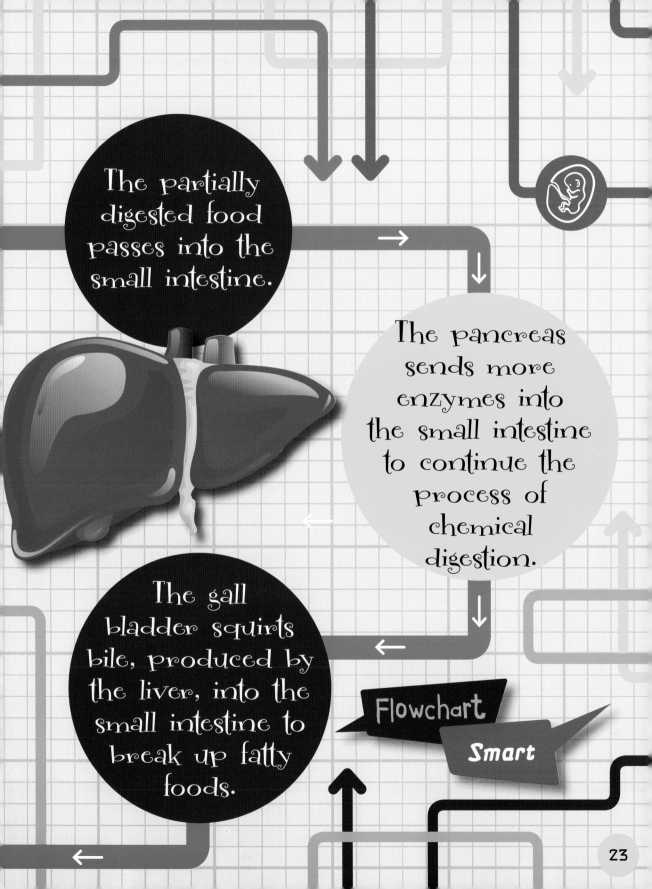

The partially digested food passes into the small intestine.

The pancreas sends more enzymes into the small intestine to continue the process of chemical digestion.

The gall bladder squirts bile, produced by the liver, into the small intestine to break up fatty foods.

Flowchart

Smart

Chapter 4
How the body uses food

After the nutrient-rich blood leaves the small intestine it is first carried to the liver. Here it is processed before being sent around the body. As well as producing bile, the liver must also separate out nutrients and toxins.

When we exercise, the liver converts some stored glycogen back into glucose to increase our energy.

Nearly all of the blood that leaves the stomach and intestines passes through the liver. The liver converts the nutrients into substances the body can use. It produces proteins and blood-clotting substances that help heal wounds in the skin. It also converts spare glucose that the body does not immediately need for energy into glycogen and stores it until it is needed.

When necessary, the liver releases glucose, proteins and other nutrients back into the blood. These are transported around the body.

The liver also helps clean the blood. It sorts and removes toxins (harmful substances) from the blood. The toxins might be pesticides that were on the food, or they might be toxins produced by the body during activities such as the breakdown of proteins. These waste substances are either carried into the bile, the small intestine, the large intestine and then out of the body, or they are carried by the blood to the kidneys.

Get smart!

If the liver does not work properly, the skin and eyes can begin to look yellow. This condition is called jaundice. Jaundice is a build-up of a substance called bilirubin in the blood and tissues. Bilirubin is a waste product created when red blood **cells** break down. It is transported to the liver and combined with bile. Jaundice can occur when the liver does not remove bilirubin from the body.

Delivering supplies

After the liver has sorted and processed nutrients and waste, it is time to deliver the particles of digested food to the body parts that need and use them. The nutrients are moved around the body in the blood by the circulatory system.

The heart is a powerful pump that squeezes blood around the body's network of blood vessels. The blood carries the nutrients to the cells of all the tissues and organs. The body's cells use different nutrients in different ways to live and grow. Cells combine glucose and **oxygen** from the blood to get energy. The liver breaks down proteins from foods such as milk, nuts and meat into separate parts called amino acids. Cells combine different amino acids to build new cells and repair damaged ones.

The heart and the main blood vessels of the circulatory system are highlighted here.

The processes that take place inside the cells also create waste. When cells use amino acids to build new cells, there is a waste product called ammonia. This can be toxic in large amounts, so it is carried in the blood away from the cells and into the liver. The liver converts the ammonia into a less harmful substance, called urea, which can be excreted from the body.

The human body is made up of millions and millions of cells. Cells are often called the building blocks of living things.

Get smart!

Blood pumped from the heart and lungs is full of oxygen that cells need to combine with glucose to release energy. As supplies run low, the blood returns to the lungs to collect more oxygen and the heart then pumps it around again. This cycle continues again and again, keeping the body's cells supplied with all the oxygen they need.

Get flow chart smart!

Nutrients and cells

Follow this flow chart to see how cells obtain and use nutrients.

Nutrient-rich blood travels from the small intestine to the liver for processing.

The liver sorts nutrients from the blood and converts them into substances the body can use.

The liver converts waste into less harmful substances, which are excreted from the body.

Nutrients are carried in the blood to cells around the body.

→

Cells combine glucose and oxygen from the blood to get energy.

Cells combine different amino acids, obtained from proteins, to build and repair cells.

↓

Waste from cell processes is carried away in the blood and into the liver.

←

Flowchart

Smart

Chapter 5
Waste

The liver is not the only organ that processes waste. The kidneys also remove waste. The kidneys are part of the body's excretory system. A quarter of your blood supply passes through your kidneys every minute.

The kidneys are two bean-shaped organs located just below the rib cage, one on each side of the backbone. Each kidney is roughly the size of an adult fist and consists of about one million filtering units called nephrons. Each nephron is so small it can only be seen with a high-powered microscope. As blood passes through the nephrons, waste is filtered from them. Cell processes create excess water and this waste is filtered from the blood by the nephrons. Other wastes include excess proteins that the body does not need.

People can live a healthy life with just one functioning kidney. If both kidneys are damaged the person may need dialysis.

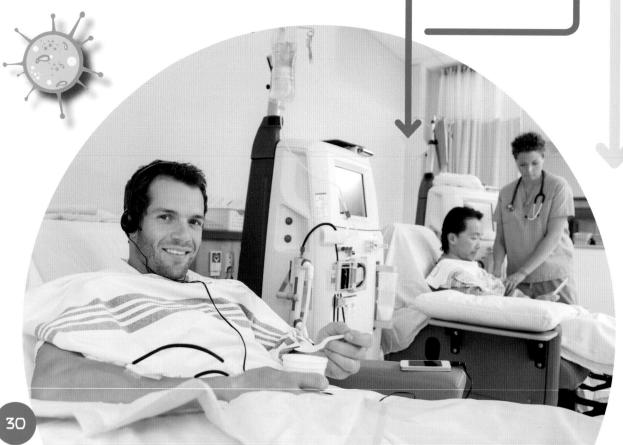

A kidney dialysis machine cleans the blood and removes excess water when a person's kidneys are not functioning properly. A tube is inserted into the person's arm. Blood is diverted out of the body and through the dialysis machine, which filters out waste products. Then the blood flows back into the person's body through a second tube. The whole process takes about 4 hours. Some patients need dialysis three or more times each week.

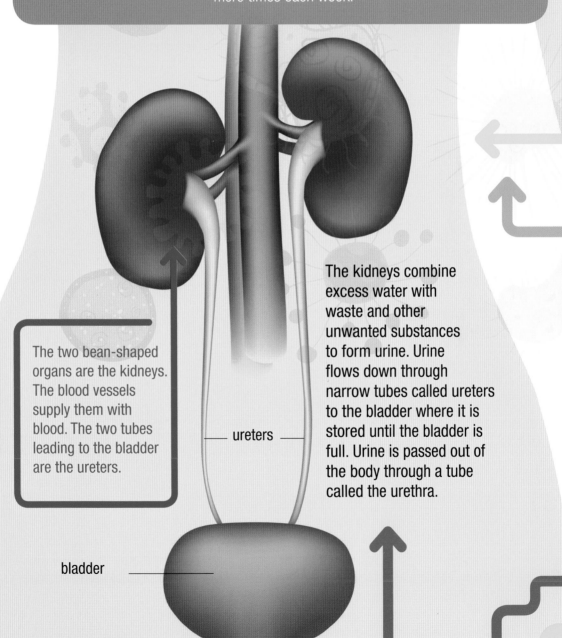

The two bean-shaped organs are the kidneys. The blood vessels supply them with blood. The two tubes leading to the bladder are the ureters.

ureters

The kidneys combine excess water with waste and other unwanted substances to form urine. Urine flows down through narrow tubes called ureters to the bladder where it is stored until the bladder is full. Urine is passed out of the body through a tube called the urethra.

bladder

Watery waste

The bladder stores urine from the kidneys. The bladder is a stretchy, round, bag-like organ that is about the size and shape of a pear when it is empty.

The walls of a hollow bladder have many folds that can open and flatten to make the bladder stretch and expand to store more urine as necessary.

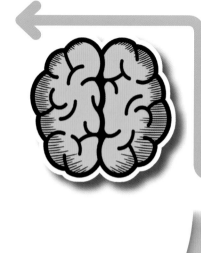

Urine is stored in the bladder until we are ready to empty it. Most people empty their bladder between 4 and 8 times a day (every 3–4 hours).

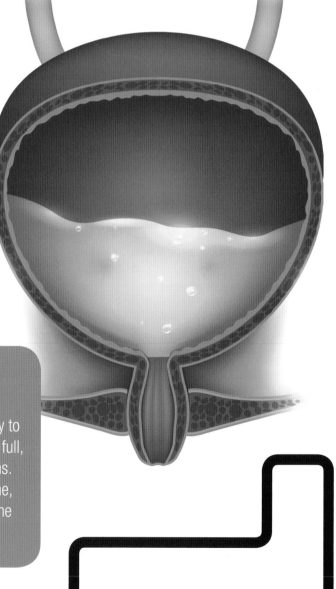

Get smart!

A bladder can increase from about 5 centimetres (2 inches) long when empty to over 15 centimetres (6 inches) long when full, depending on how much urine it contains. Although the bladder can hold more urine, the urge to urinate is usually felt when the bladder is only about one-quarter full.

When the bladder is full, nerves in the bladder wall send signals to the brain telling it that the bladder needs to be emptied. The brain sends a signal to tell us it is time to urinate. We register this as a feeling of slight discomfort.

The amount of urine a person produces depends on many factors such as the quantity of liquid they have drunk and the quantity of liquid lost as sweat. The bladder meets the urethra at rings of muscle called urethral sphincters. These sphincters are usually closed to keep any urine from leaking out. When we are ready to urinate, the brain sends signals along nerves to the sphincters telling them to relax and open. When they open, urine flows out of the bladder, down the urethra and out of the body.

An adult bladder can hold about 500 ml (1 pint) of urine before it must be emptied.

Waste disposal

By the time food mixed with digestive juices reaches the large intestine, most digestion and absorption has already taken place. The small intestine has passed almost all of the food's nutrients into the bloodstream. The large intestine's job is to absorb water and salts from undigested food and to remove any remaining waste products from the body.

The large intestine is about 1.5 metres (5 feet) long. It is a much wider tube than the small intestine. Unlike the coiled small intestine, it takes a much straighter path through your abdomen. It consists of three parts: the colon, rectum and anus. The colon is the major part of the intestine and chyme stays here for about 24 hours.

When chyme moves into the large intestine, about 90 per cent of water and almost all the nutrients have been removed from it and absorbed.

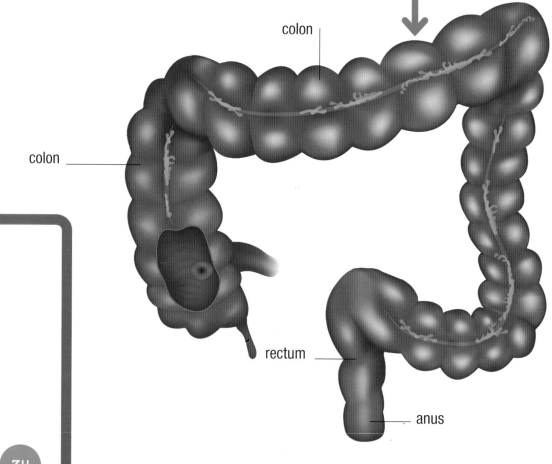

colon

colon

rectum

anus

Bacteria feed on waste material in the colon. This waste includes plant matter called fibre, which takes a long time to digest, dead cells that have shed from the lining of your intestines, salt, bile and water. The helpful bacteria not only break down waste but also produce valuable vitamins that are absorbed into your blood. As most of the remaining water is removed from the waste, the waste becomes more solid and turns into stools. The stools are stored in the rectum until the brain sends us signals that the rectum is full. Then the stools pass out of the rectum, through the anus.

Get smart!

Sometimes we pass gas from the anus. The gas is produced in the alimentary canal during the process of digestion and when bacteria in the colon break down fibre. These gases smell horrible when they contain substances such as ammonia and sulphur.

Get flow chart smart!

From the small to the large intestine

This flow chart follows the last stages of digestion when material passes from the small to the large intestine.

The small intestine removes most of the nutrients from food.

Any remaining material passes into the large intestine.

The waste is now a solid stool and it is stored in the rectum.

When the rectum is full, the stools pass out through the anus.

Bacteria in the colon of the large intestine feed on waste and undigested food.

Bacteria also produce valuable vitamins that are absorbed into the blood.

The large intestine removes most of the remaining water from the waste.

Flowchart

Smart

Chapter 6

Improving digestion

Different foods supply the body with different nutrients. Eating a variety of healthy food helps to keep the digestive system working well.

Ideally, everyone should eat at least five servings of fruit and vegetables a day. Carbohydrates in wholegrain foods such as brown bread and pasta take longer to digest, so they release energy gradually. This makes us feel full for longer. The best sources of protein are found in foods such as meat, fish, eggs and beans. There is also protein in cheese, nuts and milk, but it is important not to eat too many of these foods because they also contain a lot of fat. We need some fat, but too much can make us overweight, which is unhealthy.

When the body digests food, it releases energy that the body can use. Different activities require different amounts of energy. Sitting in front of the television uses a lot less energy than going for a bike ride or playing sport. Some foods also give the body more calories, a measure of the energy content of food, than people need. For example, processed foods such as hamburgers and chips contain a lot of calories. People become overweight when they consume more calories than their bodies use.

This plate represents the four main food groups of a balanced diet.

Some foods taste great raw, but others are better cooked. Cooking food does not just make it tastier and easier to chew. When we cook food, the heat begins to break it down before we eat it, making it easier to digest. It takes less energy for the body to digest cooked food because the process of adding heat has done some of the work already. Cooking can also kill harmful bacteria that are found in some foods.

Eating a healthy diet and doing exercise helps balance calorie intake with energy output.

Problems

The digestive system usually works efficiently, but sometimes things go wrong. A lot of the time the body recovers naturally from sickness or we can help by eating foods that keep us healthy. If you are unwell, however, it is always best to see a doctor.

People can become constipated if they do not eat enough fibre. Constipation is a painful condition in which the stools become small and hardened, making them difficult to pass. The body gets fibre from the tough parts of plants that the digestive system cannot process. Vegetables, whole grains, beans and fruits are all good sources of fibre. Fibre bulks up stools and helps them hold water. This makes them softer and easier to pass along the large intestine and out of the body.

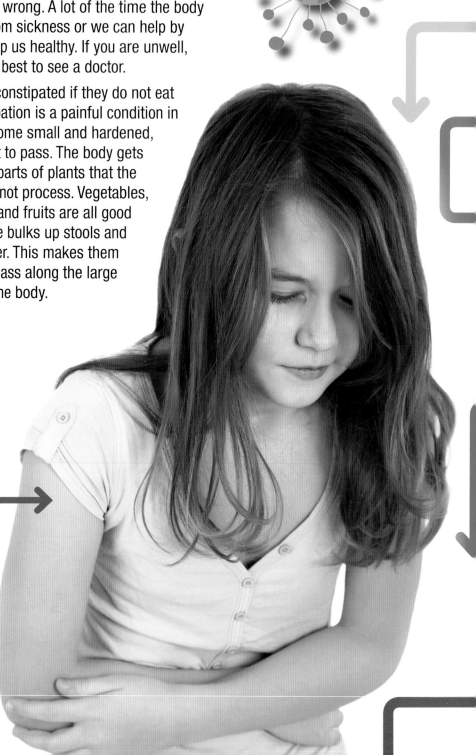

Washing your hands is a simple way to stop you catching a sickness bug.

Sometimes people accidentally eat food that contains bacteria. In other cases, bacteria or germs can enter the body when we touch dirty hands to our mouths. If you have bacteria in your stomach or intestine that are making you ill, your body makes you vomit to get rid of them. The muscles in the stomach and intestines automatically push food containing the bacteria up the oesophagus and out through the mouth. Vomit usually tastes bitter and unpleasant because it contains bile and gastric juices.

Bacteria such as this are invisible to the naked eye and can only be seen under powerful microscopes.

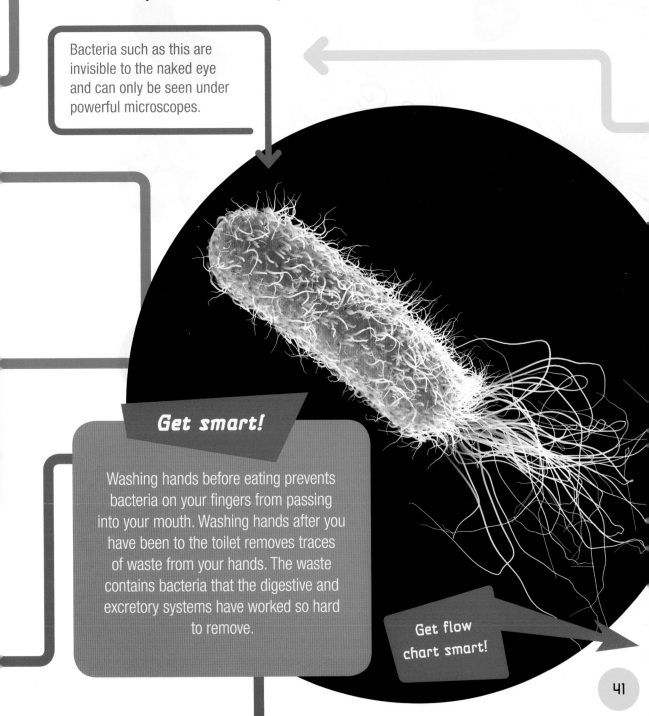

Get smart!

Washing hands before eating prevents bacteria on your fingers from passing into your mouth. Washing hands after you have been to the toilet removes traces of waste from your hands. The waste contains bacteria that the digestive and excretory systems have worked so hard to remove.

Get flow chart smart!

Bacteria

This flow chart shows how bacteria can get into our bodies and make us ill.

A girl plays in the garden and gets soil on her hands.

She does not wash her hands when she comes in for dinner.

The vomit tastes bitter and unpleasant because it contains bile and gastric juices from the stomach.

To try to remove the bacteria, muscles in the stomach and intestines push the dirty food up the oesophagus and out through the mouth. The girl vomits.

She uses her fingers to put a piece of bread into her mouth. Bacteria from the soil gets onto the food.

The bacteria travel with the food into the stomach.

Flowchart Smart

A helping hand

The digestive system is one of our most important body systems. We can help to keep it healthy. As well as eating a balanced diet containing fibre, we should try to drink plenty of water and cut down on sugary drinks.

The average human body consists of about two-thirds water. There is water in our blood, tissues and organs. We need water to stay healthy. We lose water through sweat and urination every day, so we must replace it. We also need to drink water and eat foods that contain water to keep the digestive system working. Water is necessary to help digest fibre, which helps the large intestine make soft stools that are easy to pass.

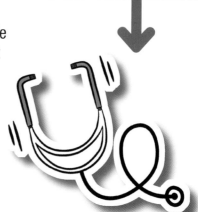

Seeds and nuts are a quick snack and a great source of fibre, which helps digestion.

Get smart!

People take antibiotics to get rid of an infection. These medicines kill both the harmful bacteria and the helpful bacteria. Eating foods such as live yogurt, sauerkraut or kimchi, which contain helpful bacteria, can help the large intestine to work efficiently again after sickness. Eating foods high in fibre helps too because high-fibre foods act as food for helpful bacteria, allowing them to grow and multiply in the digestive system.

By processing the food we eat into forms we can use, the parts and organs that make up the digestive system give us the energy and the raw materials we need to live. Without it, we could not function or survive. We should do all we can to look after our digestive system, so it can go on looking after us.

Glossary

abdomen part of the body below the chest that contains the stomach and other organs

alimentary canal parts of the body through which food moves as it is eaten and digested

calories measure of the amount of energy in food

capillaries tiny blood vessels that connect the arteries and veins

carbohydrates substances in foods that give the body energy to live and grow

cells very small parts that together form all living things

diaphragm large muscle between the chest and abdomen

digest break food down so the body can use it

dissolve break something down in liquid until it becomes part of the liquid

energy capacity to do work

enzymes chemical substances that help natural processes such as digestion

excretory system body parts that work together to remove waste from the body

gall bladder pouch near the liver that stores bile

glands organs that release chemical substances for use in the body

large intestine part of the alimentary canal that consists of the colon, rectum and anus

liver organ that removes and stores nutrients from blood and converts waste in blood into bile

molecules tiny particles of a substance made from two or more atoms

nerves fibres that carry messages between the brain and the rest of the body

oesophagus part of the alimentary canal that connects the throat to the stomach

oxygen gas in the air

pancreas organ that makes enzymes used in digestion

peristalsis rippling movement of muscles in the alimentary canal

proteins substances in some foods that the body uses to build or repair body parts

small intestine part of the alimentary canal between the stomach and the large intestine

starch carbohydrate that is the main form of stored energy in plants

surface area total area of the surface of a 3-D object

tissues groups of cells of the same type that do a job together, for example muscle cells form muscle tissues

villi tiny, finger-shaped folds in the small intestine

Find out more

Books

Human Body: A Children's Encyclopedia (DK Reference), DK (DK Children, 2012)

Nutrition: From Birth to Old Age (Your Body for Life), Robert Snedden (Raintree, 2014)

Your Digestive System: Understand it with Numbers (Your Body by Numbers), Melanie Waldron (Raintree, 2014)

Websites

Discover more about the digestive system at:
www.bbc.co.uk/guides/z9wk7p3

Find out more about digestion at:
www.dkfindout.com/uk/human-body/digestion/

Index

acids 16, 17, 18, 21

alimentary canal 12, 35

amino acids 26–27, 29

anus 12, 34, 35, 36

bacteria 17, 35, 37, 39, 41,
    42–43, 44

bile 20, 23–25, 35, 41, 42

bladder 31, 32–33

blood 5, 7, 8, 19, 22, 24, 25, 26,
    27, 28, 29, 30, 31, 34, 35,
    37, 44

capillaries 19, 22

carbohydrates 6, 9, 21, 38

cells 25, 26, 27, 28–29,
    30, 35

circulatory system 26

colon 34–35, 37

constipation 40

dialysis 31

diet 44

duodenum 19, 21

energy 6–7, 9, 18, 24, 26, 27,
    29, 38, 39, 45

enzymes 10, 17, 18, 21, 22, 23

excretory system 5, 8,
    30, 41

fats 6, 7, 9, 20, 21, 23, 38

fibre 35, 40, 44

gall bladder 20, 23

gastric juices 17, 21, 41, 42

glands 10, 14, 17

glucose 7, 18, 24, 25, 26, 27,
    29

glycogen 24

ileum 19

jaundice 25

jejunum 19

kidneys 25, 30–31, 32

large intestine 12, 14, 19, 25,
    34, 36–37, 40, 44

liver 20, 23, 24–25, 26, 27, 28,
    29, 30

mouth 10, 12, 13, 14, 41, 42,
    43

mucus 21

muscle 12, 16, 22, 33,
    41, 42

nerves 33

nutrients 5, 8, 12, 15, 19, 22,
    24, 25, 26, 28–29,
    34, 36

oesophagus 11, 12, 13, 15, 16,
    41, 42

pancreas 20, 21, 23

peristalsis 12

plants 7, 35, 40

photosynthesis 7

proteins 6, 9, 17, 21, 24, 25,
    26, 29, 30, 38

rectum 34, 35, 36

saliva 10, 14

small intestine 12, 15, 18–19,
    20, 21, 22–23, 24, 25, 28,
    34, 36

starch 7, 10, 14

stomach 11, 12–13, 15, 16–17,
    18, 20, 21, 22, 24, 41, 42,
    43

tongue 10, 11, 15

urine 31, 32–33

villi 18–19, 22

vitamins 6, 7, 9, 19, 35, 37

vomit 41, 42

waste 5, 8, 12, 14, 25, 26, 27,
    28, 29, 30–31, 32, 34, 35,
    36, 37, 41